chartered
management
institute

inspiring leaders

The leading organisation for professional management

As the champion of management, the Chartered Management Institute shapes and supports the managers of tomorrow. By sharing intelligent insights and setting standards in management development, the Institute helps to deliver results in a dynamic world.

Setting and raising standards

The Institute is a nationally accredited organisation, responsible for setting standards in management and recognising excellence through the award of professional qualifications.

Encouraging development, improving performance

The Institute has a vast range of development programmes, qualifications, information resources and career guidance to help managers and their organisations meet new challenges in a fast-changing environment.

Shaping opinion

With in-depth research and regular policy surveys of its 91,000 individual members and 520 corporate members, the Chartered Management Institute has a deep understanding of the key issues. Its view is informed, intelligent and respected.

For more information call 01536 204222 or visit www.managers.org.uk

CONTENTS

Foreword   5

Introduction   6

Sunday   A wider Web market   9

Monday   The webmarketing.com mix   18

Tuesday   Web business tactics   40

Wednesday   Your web home   61

Thursday   Web research   71

Friday   Web copy   81

Saturday   Climbing higher   90

For Michelle and Joshua
– with love and admiration

Special thanks to my brother Raphael for being the first to
show me the potential of IT

Liz Ross for her professionalism, The Chartered
Management Institute and Sun Microsystems

When the first edition of this book came out, the world was a very different place. Just about everyone believed that by merely adding dotcom to a company name, any commercial potential would have unlimited prospects for growth.

Hardware manufacturers saw unprecedented growth. Internet consultants prophesied about a 'brave new world – without frontiers'. Referring to the first edition of this book, Sun Microsystems said, 'Webmarketing is a challenge we should embrace now, from dotcom-ing your whole communications strategy to creating an interactive website.' It was reminiscent of a Wild West boom town. Then, the Internet bubble finally burst. Many dotcoms became notcoms.

Even with much talk of boom and bust, all was far from doom and gloom. The failures taught businesses, tough, yet crucial long-term lessons. The result of those lessons was three-fold. Firstly, the very best dotcoms survived and even flourished. Secondly, the dotcom revolution gave a shot of confidence to every kind of business person and aspiring entrepreneur to 'have a go'. In marketing – 'having a go' is the fodder for success for those who dare to tread where competitors simply dip their toes.

Finally, irrespective of the initial dotcom hype, thanks to the Internet, like it or not, the world changed irreversibly. Today's connected communities offer marketers the greatest ever opportunities to reach local markets on a global level – at home, work and even on the move – not on terms dictated by corporations but led by consumers, clients and surfers alike – the marketplace.

Without hype or jargon, this book introduces you to the principles of web marketing. Its foundations help take your ideas onto the global stage. This doesn't just take luck – it calls for successful web marketing that starts in a week and endures for a lifetime.

JJ Gabay
jj@gabaynet.com

Technology has always helped markets develop. The railways brought commerce into small communities, the telephone crossed vast plains, the car gave mobility, the computer saved time, and now e-commerce and the custodian of its message – webmarketing – combines all kinds of communications whilst offering immense market potentials.

Like all industries starting in the kindergarten of enthusiasts and ending as part of the essential rules used in the playground of life, webmarketing's possibilities are enormous. We've reached less than twenty percent of the Internet's potential marketing value. The extent of the Internet will spread widely at an incredible pace. By 2010, wireless technology will become second nature to virtually all mobile phone users and even car drivers with in built display modems in their vehicles' dashboards. Not forgetting web links via televisions at home and connections via sophisticated game consoles. Rapid access speeds via broadband connections will soon be commonplace. If the motor industry shared the computer industry's rate of growth since 1990, at today's prices a car would cost no more than £1.93.

So long as there is a demand for products and services, marketing will continue to evolve its methodology according to the available resources that enable organisations like yours meet market needs. Webmarketing provides today's web-wide marketing solutions for a planet made up of multifarious business communities. Each organisation forming an integral part of those communities needs profitable ways to take advantage of what has become a wired economy.

■ I N T R O D U C T I O N ■

Today's language of marketing communication relies heavily on the manner in which you disseminate mission-critical information. With the so-called dotcom era, the world is as small as a microchip with marketing opportunities that are equally intricate. The marketing implications of dotcom business solutions are extensive:

- Local values become international issues affecting your marketing plan
- Preparation assumes greater significance
- Your promotions, including direct and awareness marketing, integrate with your total business aspirations
- Campaigns are information-led, driven by customer needs.

Webmarketed projects get to market faster. Costs to reach your internal as well as external markets are incrementally reduced. Clicks and mortar replace bricks and mortar. In so doing, small business can flourish as well as the bigger players, whilst serving community needs – thus aiding the 'smart growth' economy.

Moreover, despite all its perceived complexity, *dotcom's* business clarity ensures that in practice you no longer have to study to be a computer technologist. Instead, you become a marketing technologist, using a mix of traditional, contemporary and visionary tools.

■ I N T R O D U C T I O N ■■

Over the next seven days you'll learn how to combine your own marketing mix with the dotcom paradigm.

We'll be looking at:

- The evolution of webmarketing
- How webmarketing adapts to your audience
- How to promote a webbrand
- How to plan a Web-based business
- How to integrate your web needs with your customer's desires and suppliers infrastructures
- How to conduct a Web-wide research project
- The secrets behind successful web-advertising
- The synergy between traditional marketing and webmarketing
- How to establish a practical webmarketing strategy
- Why you should build a web portal
- What to look for in a website
- How to chose your ideal ISP
- How to produce creative web copy
- How to get your site ranked at the top of a search engine

A wider Web market

The wider Web makes the world a narrower place.
Geographic borders are less defined. Deadlines, shorter.
International time and distance is as relative as the space
between your keyboard and fingertips.

As you read these words, businesses are saving billions of
dollars for themselves and their customers through
implementing e-commerce sales cycles. For example, vast
transportation cost savings are made by comparing logistic
tenders by countries on-line.

Despite the initially shaky start, the Internet is the thirteenth
biggest economy in the world. It's no longer just websites,
e-commerce, e-solutions or area networks – webmarketing
is business and everything attached to it, from mobile
phones to music centres.

For all this technology, businesses still rely on targeted,
value-added sales propositions to draw in new customers
whilst securing existing ones. Webmarketing techniques
strengthen relationships with stockholders, employees
and suppliers. It touches every aspect of your marketing
mix, from sales and distribution to advertising (see
Monday). In so doing, webmarketing positively
distinguishes your organisation from that of your
competitors. As we progress through this week you will
see how.

Explosive e-business

At the time of writing, every four seconds a further eleven organisations establish an Internet presence thereby linking to the world's most successful, broadly spread communications network – the World Wide Web. By 2005, worldwide more than 500 million people will be surfing the Web, from 'Teeny Techies' (aged 6–16) to 'Silver Surfers' (aged 50+).

The popularity of the Internet is only part of a bigger webmarketing picture. Yet, just taking the Internet, you can measure its incredible growth in a relatively short time scale.

wEB FACTs

IT TOOK 38 YEARS FOR RADIO TO ATTRACT 50 MILLION
LISTENERS AND 13 YEARS FOR TELEVISION TO ATTRACT 50
MILLION VIEWERS.

IN JUST 4 YEARS THE INTERNET ATTRACTED 50 MILLION
SURFERS!

Those figures can hardly be balked at, especially when you
consider the Internet's beginnings.

Less is more

A key business concept during the 90s was
'disintermediation': cutting out middlemen in complex
markets. Typically, the scissors were the web and other
digital media. As tools, Intranets and Extranets managed
corporate internal affairs. Floppy discs went into Zip speed.
Tape videos forwarded into video and audio streamed
media Web pages. Cumbersome PCs stepped into small
footprint workstations. Mini-Discs shrunk into earphone
MP3 Players, hand held phones fitted into pocket shirts.
TV's turned into digital entertainment centres and diaries
became wireless palm held devices, ready to download
webpages into the hands of a mobile target audience. The
stage was set, the network was switched on: the dotcom
connected age had arrived.

Who is on-line and why?

Today's customers expect businesses to provide goods and services quickly and efficiently and at a location that suits their requirements *more conveniently than yours*. This kind of thinking is a two-way street. Just as your customers and trading partners need to sense that they are in control so you too need to have firm control of your Web business.

The internal audience

As with traditional marketing, your audience is split into distinctive camps: the internal audience and the external audience.

Both are vital. Your internal audience comprises a community of employees, suppliers, distributors, sales force, consultants, and so on, who typically connect to you via a distributed computing network like a secure Intranet. This internal enterprise-wide network uses the same TCP (Transmission Control Protocol) Internet Protocol technology as the Internet. Using Web browsers, an Intranet network directs information from both the World Wide Web and internal systems to individual company PCs. To prevent unauthorised access by anyone on the World Wide Web, the system is shielded from the outside world by security software called a 'firewall'.

The virtual company bulletin board
In addition to being a tremendous internal communication tool, Intranets can save significant marketing print costs through disseminating anything from a newsletter to internal telephone directory, all of which can be updated regularly.

The external audience

To communicate with external partners like suppliers and sales outlets, you could use an Extranet. This takes a network group of computers beyond the boundaries of an office. It sort of hitches a ride on the back of the World Wide Web using the same electronic dialogue protocols of the Internet. Obviously information is subject to passwords and the network is not open to the general public.

Web tip
Check that your site – internal or Internet-wide – prints. Just because a page is on the screen, it doesn't mean it will download to an office printer.

Web community

Your external surfers are individuals:

- *Prospective buyers* – anyone in the right demographic and with appropriate requirements who can be encouraged to contact your enterprise.
- *Existing customers* – who have previously dealt with you.
- *Borderline customers* – who may leave unless you improve your sales support.
- *Lapsing customers* – who want new services.
- *Potential clients* – who, having previously bought goods, can be encouraged to buy more.
- *Media* – such as trade and national press journalists who want 'real time' access to today's news rather than yesterday's headlines.
- *Potential employees* – who want published information.
- *Partners* – teaming up with your organisation and able to distribute your products electronically.
- *Would-be investors* – who want solid corporate facts as well as reassuring, visionary communications.
- *Allies* – who'll recommend you to others, especially if motivated with an incentive.

Which web medium suits you?

Web benefit	Intranet	Extranet	Web vehicle
Strengthen partnerships		✓	
Create loyalty programmes		✓	www
Build brand awareness			www
Increase business efficiencies	✓	✓	
On-line company manuals	✓		www email Bulletin Board System (BBS)
On-line product demonstrations	✓	✓	www
On-line departmental conference links via webcams	✓	✓	www
On-line newsletter	✓	✓	www email
On-line recruitment	✓		www
On-line precision direct marketing	✓	✓	www
On-line sales training	✓	✓	
On-line ordering		✓	www email Electronic Data Information (EDI)
On-line project tracking	✓	✓	Agent software EDI
On-line product catalogue		✓	www

Web benefit	Intranet	Extranet	Web vehicle
On-line support	√	√	BBS email www
Mobile/home working computing/ laptop sales links	√		www BBS
Cross-company selling (e.g. Airline ticketing agency linking with a hotel chain)		√	www email
Enhanced customer and employee relationships	√	√	www
Inventory control	√		Agent software email EDI

Retaining attention

The minute your site is accessed by a potential customer, you have around 20 to 40 seconds to retain attention. Failure to do so means your potential customers remain just that – potential.

To keep them on-line longer, you will need to understand the systems which secure your webmarketing presence such as equipment, Internet Service Providers, website maintenance distribution and so forth. Even if you are only concerned with the shop-front part of your website – at the very least, you need to understand why a consumer would want to visit your page. Keeping them hooked takes strong personalisation in what is, superficially, a highly impersonal mass broadcast media.

Summary

People access the Web to share ideas globally. They become part of the overall context of the message being conveyed and so share the experience of your web brand.

The greater the number of targeted surfers who log on to a website for a trusted brand, the higher the so called 'eyeball' share. To retain a surfer's attention you need to tailor and support a brand experience. The first way to establish trust of a web brand is through security assurance. Technologies to protect data over the web are improving by the month. Initiatives from credit card companies to underwrite purchases over the Internet are ensuring that people feel more confident when dealing on-line with their favourite brands.

Web brands are also taking advantage of greater bandwidths for faster downloads – reassurance for surfers who expect a prompt and relevant service from their favoured web brand.

In terms of on-screen advertising, rich media banner ads increase web brand awareness in a one-to-one dynamic environment. Rather than simply promoting a webbrand on a static banner advertisement, information is being disseminated and subsequent sales secured instantly at the click of a mouse.

Finally, however great your web brand may appear on the screen, the ability to fulfil orders promptly through improved distribution systems ensures that surfers come back.

The more people linked to your network, the greater the opportunities to reach micro-communities with highly specialised interests.

The webmarketing.com mix

Today we explore how webmarketing affects your traditional marketing mix.

Business objective	Traditional marketing	Webmarketing	Future marketing
Segmentation	Demographic lifestyle	Behaviour	Complex data
Recruitment	Advertising/agent	On-line	Direct cabled or wireless access to prospective employees.
Positioning	Local/national broadcasting/ publishing	Local understanding – global awareness	Service segmentation according to customer needs
Advertising	'Pulling' customers to the message	'Pushing' the message to customers	Empowering customers to 'push' or 'pull' at will
Education	Content led	Content and context led	Interactive
Distribution	Middle man	On-line – on target	One to one
Media	By classification	By interoperable platform	By digital and newer technologies
Administration	Paper based	Wire based	Multi-media based

Business objective	Traditional marketing	Webmarketing	Future marketing
Branding	Market share	Share of customer 'eye-ball' share – number of surfers	Mind share – Or via web browsing, 'search-share'
Market reach	Geographic	Webgraphic	Intellectual ingress

Marketing integration

Until recently, whenever marketers featured the Internet or indeed any computing application as part of the marketing mix, the lead was placed firmly in the hands of technical system integrators. Today, you have to be a marketing communications integrator. In doing so, decide from a practical business view how the Internet helps establish, maintain and enrich your market's attention ('eyeball share') and, ultimately, allegiance.

To be implemented successfully, webmarketing needs to be:

- *planned* with your own aspirations in mind
- *organised* in collaboration with technicians
- *designed* in agreement with management goals: these could include extending your product life cycle or increasing the share of your customers or total market
- *managed* to enhance the long-term relationship between your organisation and its public
- *directed* by your marketing team, supported by technicians
- *measured* according to time, value, aspirations as well as management intent.

If you are not completely sure of what your webmarketing campaign should achieve, you'll invariably end up with a compromise of several half-hearted stabs rather than a precise hit.

The Boston Matrix

Every service or product coming onto a market can be categorised into one of four quadrants within a framework called 'The Boston Matrix'. The vertical axis of the box represents market growth, whilst the horizontal shows market share. Growth varies according to market demands and economic conditions. Companies falling in the best performing part of the matrix have products with a high market growth and share. These are called 'Stars'. Those with high market share but low growth are 'Cash cows'. In cases of low market share but growing as a whole, you get 'problem children' (also known as 'Wildcats' or 'Question marks'). Products struggling with low market share and growth are 'Dogs'.

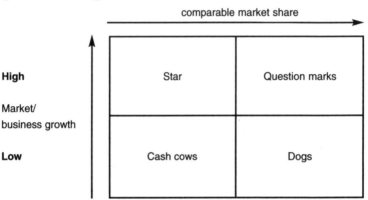

The classic Boston matrix

Carving your webshare

Here's the conventional model adapted and updated for today's webmarketing trends.

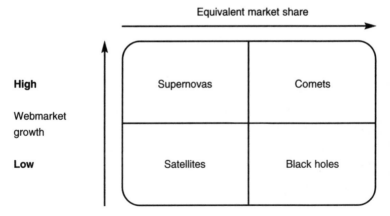

The modern Web matrix

To a greater or lesser extent, your web brand portfolio will spread across one or more segments.

Black holes
'Black Holes', the equivalent of 'Dogs', produce relatively little cash flow. If they are part of an external market, 'Black hole' surfers typically skim through sites at two clicks per page, occasionally lingering. However, that's as far as they go.

Satellites
If your web product or service enters Satellite web space, you'll be in the company of enterprises enjoying regular Internet traffic. As WWW watchers, 'satellite' surfers may visit sites offering services like books on-line, or audio/MP3 (audio file compression). As the market is mature, add value through enhancements such as useful information repositories or webcams at important events.

Satellites should be rewarded with beneficial features and values that they would naturally expect from your brand as conveyed in traditional advertising but reinterpreted for the web age.

Useful web innovations for Satellite markets may include:

- Free software to enhance printing of web pages
- Personalised Internet ordering
- Ongoing recommendations at discounted prices.

Comets
Comet sites may feature all the latest enhancements, but you'll still need to invest heavily in PR, links to other sites,

as well as traditional advertising, to increase market share in what is a very fickle sector.

Supernovas
Supernovas are at the pinnacle of webmarkets. Popular search engines like Yahoo are Supernovas. However, be forewarned – competing organisations are always at your heels. For Internet Service Providers (ISPs), this includes delivering '24–7' support. For Internet businesses, ensure the backbone infrastructure, such as servers and software for internal networks as well as external, is current.

Is the Internet *really* profitable?

At the launch of the music company *MP3.com* on the stock market, the company was valued at 4.5 billion dollars. Yet by its third month, it had lost 1.5 million. That's not as gloomy as you may think. Internet companies are still brave pioneers. They, and hopefully you, are building the infrastructure and new commercial ethics of what in just a few years will be the dotcom standard. For now, economists value web companies by 'burn-rate' – the amount they lose. The idea is that the more money they lose, the more they have to lose – so the bigger they are! At the time of writing, the biggest webstore is Amazon.com.

Get web branding

The pace of the Internet is forcing brand leaders to reassess their strategies in a bid to turn current modest brands into future global icons.

70% of European Internet users buying online by 2004.

Total European online ordering population will increase from 19 million in 2000 to 100 million in 2004.

100% per year e-commerce growth until 2003
$1.5 trillion European online sales in 2004.

Europe's major contributor to the global Internet economy will reach $6.9 trillion in 2004.

By 2005 e-commerce will account for 7% of Europe's retail sales. In Northern Europe the gap with the US may be entirely closed, with the US falling behind in some categories.

Source – Datamonitor/Forestter

Thanks to the Internet's ability to personalise a global branding positioning, webmarketing helps globally respected names become more relevant for local markets. The greater a web brand's relevance, the more it reflects consumer aspirations and values. There are ten stages to founding powerful web brands:

1 Establish a market need
2 Create market awareness by addressing that need
3 Form a point of distinction between you and your competitors
4 Make your brand memorable on the Internet – so it becomes a resource
5 Demonstrate value added innovations that enhance your basic fulfilment proposition

6 Encourage customer loyalty rather than one-off 'click and buy' sales opportunities
7 Support brand values with promotions, including press, banner advertising, PR and direct marketing
8 Re-invigorate your brand according to market conditions – without compromising your competitive point of difference
9 Offer a broad bandwidth to make your brand accessible
10 Support your web brand presence with traditional marketing techniques.

The next generation
'First generation' sites purely supplied previously published marketing information and company background information. This included lists of products and financial status. These were, and still are, known as 'brochureware'.

Your Web presence should offer accessible and useful additional support and services to your market. However, if you want to feature your corporate brochure as part of a website, divide its content into logical sections, then save those sections as PDF files. As you've divided the brochure into manageable 'chunks,' downloading won't freeze your surfer's computer.

Web tip
Save pictures that don't have to be bigger than 25% of your individual web pages as low-resolution graphics. This improves downloading. Also, avoid complicated graphics for backgrounds. Pale colours work best.

Step	Internet	Extranet	Intranet
1. *Brochureware*	Cost effective publishing	Gets material to key people faster	Easy to control
2. *Add interactive features* e.g. email	Encourages a simple relationship	Lets you issue/ take simple instructions	Develops existing email infrastructures
3. *Replace cumbersome distribution systems with web-based processes* e.g. on-line payments	Shortens time to market	Saves on administration	Encourages mobile computing on the road or at different locations
4. *Replace two-step systems with total web-based processes* e.g. distribution management	Offers a fast, tailored delivery service for customers on a global scale	Employs 'Just In Time' management techniques – this delays ordering goods from suppliers or warehouses until there is sufficient customer demand, so saving stock holding and handling costs	Saves on manpower

Four steps of Web business evolution

The volume of information on the Internet tends to expand according to the number of people connected to the network (currently on target to reach 600 million by 2005). This throws up all kinds of implications:

- Specific information becomes harder to track down as it is drowned in a sea of facts
- The integrity of the information becomes increasingly dubious as anyone can publish anything
- The demand for information imposes significant pressure on technology to keep communication channels 'open' and 'flowing'.

Address these issues and you'll be on the way to being respected as a valuable web brand.

Webmarketing support tools

In addition to Internet marketing techniques which elevate your information up the ranks of traditional 'spider' search engines (see Saturday's chapter), consider less obvious yet essential webmarketing support tools.

For example, use software which manipulates and keeps your information relevant to your market. Equally, have an appropriate army of servers or datacenters. These computers deliver services to other computers on your network. Simple datacenter technology keeps everyone on-line thus ensuring that your marketing communication remains accessible, secure and available.

Get to the point
When dealing with either internal or external Internet markets, it is imperative that your site is designed not to lose surfers by thrusting complex mazes of 'dead-end' information at them.

Pornography sites, accounting for ten per cent of web pages and worth around $1 billion a year, are renowned for this. According to industry figures, in 2002 workers were spending 91 minutes a month viewing around 409 different pages. Just over half the time was spent devoted to viewing pornography.

Typically, pornography sites throw up page after page of the equivalent of brick walls. When 'clicked', these lead to further sister pages, ultimately returning to the original content page. 'Regular' sites far too often use this incestuous activity. Such unwieldy Internet features are called Octopus or Loose-End sites. Avoid building them.

Web brands – supporting your brand message

Arguably, external market facing sites that deal directly with customers, thus cutting out the middle person, alienate your conventional sales channel. Not true. Your website can be used as an advertising support mechanism rather than a direct sales device. For instance, you could run a press advertisement for a new range of clothing. Meanwhile, you decide to generate traffic to your website. So the advertisement features your WWW address.

If, having accessed your site, all the surfer sees is an animated version of the same advertisement, you would have wasted a customer's time. However, if for example the site features a virtual catwalk of models wearing your range of clothing, you add real value. Add the addresses of local retailers and you will also keep your sales channel happy.

You may want to go the full distance by selling directly on the superhighway. This kind of e-commerce is simply another outlet that provides convenience for customers. Your traditional sales channel needn't worry too much. There will always be a demand for the sales cycle of some products and services to be completed in person. Even if your site doesn't generate instant sales, with the right exposure it still generates awareness.

Supporting your brand message, and so the profit potential of terrestrial retailers, is one of the Web's finer attributes. Newspapers and magazines use the Internet to offer up-to-the-minute coverage of news, or to provide an on-line search of previously published articles. In doing so, the paper reaches an audience beyond the familiar news-stand. Many broadcasters offer free access to the Internet, not to generate immediate sales but to spread web brand awareness.

Service companies can demonstrate that a brand is 'fresh' in its approach towards individualising its portfolio of benefits for customers. For example, insurance companies often offer personalised quotations via the Internet.

One thing that should always be borne in mind – building an on-line shop is quite different from building a web brand. On-line shopping is about selling at every opportunity, even after the goods have been 'placed' in the electronic shopping cart. For example, rewarding the surfer for their custom with further discounts. Or recommending products to previous customers based on their preferences or buying patterns. While the shopping experience should be based on retailing principles, reflecting marketing strategies, the brand experience should be based on marketing strategies which, depending on your long term goals, may or may not be manifested through an on-line shop.

wEB FACTs

ACCORDING TO MORI, 10% OF ALL UK SURFERS DESCRIBE THEMSELVES AS REGULAR ON-LINE SHOPPERS. THIS FIGURE TENDS TO DOUBLE EVERY YEAR.

Marketing platforms

Software such as Java, Sun Microsystem's universally adopted mother tongue of network computing, lets you 'push' your marketing message through any platform or device including PCs, Macs, workstations, UNIX machines, network computers, set-top boxes, palm held devices, wrist watches or cellular phones.

To ensure that your message reaches your mobile audience, using WAP and GPRS – as well as 3G technology you could sponsor a mobile news service for cellular users. News can be accessed initially in a text message form. While the mobile phone user is reading the latest news, your message could be transmitted and personalised according to the location of the phone, for example you run a restaurant chain and want to direct mobile phone users towards your nearest restaurant. Loyalty is often influenced by convenience, so this kind of personalisation enhances your business. It all amounts to further integrity for your organisation and bigger dotcom business opportunities all round.

Enterprise Information Portals

The fusion of traditional marketing and new media establishes even more powerful web brands – some of which start life on the Web. Micro net companies operating from a small office may use the Web to reach national or even international markets. As with all markets, the enterprises that offer the best value in terms of cost, audience appropriateness, service and access ultimately squeeze out the competition. The current trend is for large, established off-line brands to develop so-called 'Enterprise Information Portals'. These lead to anything related to the portal's theme, such as news or fashion brand sites.

In a nutshell, portals provide content from multiple sources. Themed portals evolved from Search Engines that traditionally pointed the surfer to any site with registered details. Portals generate targeted 'hits' and cash for website owners who:

1 want to be listed on the portal
2 want to advertise on a portal's banner space.

wEB FACTs

SOME PUBLISHERS USE PORTALS TO CAPTURE 'CYBERGRAPHIC' DATA. THIS MAY INCLUDE TRACKING HOW MANY 30-YEAR-OLD FEMALES VISIT A SPECIFIC SITE. WHAT DO THEY BUY, AND SO ON? THIS INFORMATION IS FURTHER ANALYSED FOR WOULD-BE INTERNET AND PRINT ADVERTISERS.

Portal flavours

A so called 'horizontal portal' presents information organised according to categories. Surfers are induced to return to such horizontal portals through associated services like investment market news, music news and so on.

Typically, a horizontal portal features:

- Web searching
- reference-news guides
- on-line shopping
- freebies like email and community networking.

To further seduce surfers to a horizontal portal, many have negotiated with browsers like Netscape and Explorer to feature a special 'My Portal' button, eg 'My Yahoo'. When 'clicked' the surfer arrives at a specific portal.

The surfer can customise all such links to ensure receipt of a daily horoscope for instance. If precisely targeted, horizontal portals offer webmarketers invaluable direct marketing opportunities. Some webmarketers offer part of their site content to portals in exchange for links. For instance, newspapers may offer headline news in exchange for promoting the portal's URL in their publication and website. If you are going to consider a link exchange, simply send an email to prospective link sites clearly explaining your URL and offer to link.

> **Web tip**
> Similar to portals, a 'trailblazer site' leads to useful support companies and tools via hypertext links. The better the tools, the greater your credibility as a valuable resource.

Vertical portals
Vertical portals are so individual that in some instances they are adapted as corporate specific Intranet portals, carrying a secure flow of company-wide information. The same idea works for Extranet business-to-business portals.

Thanks to thin-client computing architecture, the whole process of setting up portals is more affordable than ever. Thin-client computers don't require disk storage, applications or even operating systems. So they can include devices like mobile phones, screen phones and handheld organisers. All the essential information and software resides on a server, ready to be delivered as required to any Java protocol-enabled client.

Another benefit from vertical portals is that rather than investing large sums in advertising on search engine owned portals, you can build your own portal presence.

Portals – controlling your internal market

Portal technology offers fast, secure access to personal email, data, applications, internal sites and network services from any Internet-connected device. The entire environment is web-enabled, so there are vast savings when upgrading individual applications. You no longer need to build a virtual private network. Research shows that it costs two and half times more a year to support 2,000 remote access users using traditional remote access infrastructures than through Internet remote access.

The right portal supplier can show ways to allow authorised users like employees to securely access network resources via a standard browser on any Internet-connected device like a palm or laptop computer. The business benefit of this is that you remain in total control of who enters from the Internet and what they can access. There's no need for special client software. Extranet business partners (behind a firewall) can also access authorised partner applications from any device with Internet abilities.

Portals – What is suitable for your business?
Decide which level of portal sophistication is appropriate for your business needs.

Simple
- Company information
- Product and service data
- Search

Fundamental
- Company information

- Advanced Search
- Product and service data
- Company-wide directories
- Complex information
- Personalisation

Elaborate
- Company information
- Complex information
- Company-wide directories
- Customer support
- Channel collaboration
- Product and service data
- Advanced search
- Personalisation
- Transactions
- Personalised work management

Premium
- Supply support chain management
- Advance personalisation
- EDI (Electronic Data Interchange) stock control, with links directly to suppliers
- Java and associated software enabling

Web brand or fad?

A web brand has to be more than a 'fad'. Left under-marketed, the average life cycle for a web brand is from nine weeks to just under nine months.

How can you measure the power of your web brand?

- **Web brand extent**: integration of traditional brand values with Internet enabled technologies
- **Web brand breadth**: market sector admiration through utilising Internet technologies to enhance perceived brand benefits
- **Web brand influence**: the relevance the webbrand attracts from various market segments, including employees via intranets, suppliers via Extranets and shareholders via WWW
- **Web brand affinity**: the allegiance your webbrand attracts from existing as well as likely customers
- **Web brand alliance**: the degree of feeling and emotions evoked by your web brand.

Enduring web brands understand markets. In so doing, they enhance the conduct of web business. This includes the management of bandwidth issues. After all, no one wants to wait minutes for a web advert to download. It also means doing more than just plastering pages with brand logos. Such icons alone (that can't be identified by search engines) have no substance. Customers won't wait. Your brand may capture attention, but simply on its own it may not encourage loyalty.

This brand value approach extends to the placement and rationale of banner advertisements. There's no point featuring a banner ad if, once clicked, it doesn't lead anywhere that is relevant to the original content of the page or site where it first appeared.

New e-conomics mix

Product

On-line support

Consistent reviews

Clearly designed (Web page)

Highly interactive

Surfer/customer-centric rather than corporate-centric

Place

Electronic distribution

Greater control of your supply management chain via: www.

Email

Intranet

Internet

Extranet

Improved enterprise-wide communication via Network computing devices: mobile phones.

Laptop computers.

Desktop computers

New customer value added opportunities via Jini activated household appliances (e.g. intelligent fridges, cookers)

Web screen phones

Electronic kiosks

People

Innovation

Vision

Dynamism

Logic

Style

Intuition

Technical Competence

Price

Secure credit card payment

Direct debit

Local billing

Promotion and e-branding

WWW offers

Brand-led site imagery

Intranet employee offers

Web banners

'Push-mail' (you send updates, rather than wait for enquiries)

On-line sales (customer sales enhancements' e.g. electronic 'shopping carts')

Posters

Press advertising

Radio

TV

Direct mail

Web-shots

Web page sponsorship

Web newsletters

Process

Bandwidth management

Distribution

Ordering cycles

> **Web tip**
> Make 85% of your web strategy value-led and 15%
> sales oriented.

The Four Ps

The original marketing mix, coined by Jerome McCarthy,
was known as, 'the 'Four Ps'. This was amended to the
'Five Ps + *People*' and then 'Six Ps + *Process*'.

As no market ever stands still, the mix is constantly re-balanced
as the e-conomics mix demonstrates.

- Design your company around customers' needs
- Maintain dialogue
- Customise products and services
- Think beyond core product, ie more about the total
  customer experience and needs
- Don't fear organisational change – embrace it
- Manage your business in real time and offer 24 hour
  service
- Use the Internet to expand brand values and/or
  build an entirely new brand
- Expect change, plan and react accordingly
- Learn new skills – what you know is more important
  than what you own
- Use the Internet to reduce development time of new
  products and services

- Streamline the supply chain (Enterprise Resource Planning – ERP, which helps optimise every link in your chain)
- Offer greater customer convenience
- Wire your company for profits – consider customer imperatives and use your IT infrastructure to service external needs.

Web business basics

Irrespective of whether or not you want webmarketing to increase short-term profits, mid to long term there is a very high chance that it will save money for your company. However, many companies still spend months deciding whether or not to go on-line. Below are some of the key benefits of taking the first steps:

Key business benefit of the Web:	Practical ideas:
Helps you reach new markets	Conduct global business 24–7
Aids your market research	• Generate 'real time' opinion polls • Create on-line focus groups • Brainstorm ideas with local markets • Gain a complete 360° view of prospective as well as existing customers.
Generates sales leads	• Direct enquiries from Web pages to local dealers • Support your global branding strategy • Reach directly into the offices and homes of your marketplace • Distribute CD ROMs which guide prospects around your portfolio – and link directly to websites.
Offers pre-sales support	• Publish brochureware • Offer credit term details • Provide direct email access between sales staff and potential clients • Generate interactive Web-showrooms • Empower customers to help themselves.

Key business benefit of the Web:	Practical ideas:
Offers post-sales support	• Profit from on-line technical support • Build customer retention through rapid response to on-going enquiries • Link with business-to-business partners to deliver a seamless service to end-users, e.g. by integrating airline ticket reservations with hotel reservations.
Enhances your brand image	• Adopt new technologies such as streaming video and audio ideal, for example, when addressing shareholders. Instead of just publishing an annual report you could also Web-publish a movie clip of your chairperson's speech.
Improves your direct marketing	• Target people by age, occupation etc.
Strengthens your media relations	• Send press releases by email incorporating video clips of your product and service. Or subscribing to powerful news clipping sources that deliver real time news. • Link with news companies to provide access to news from your home page which ultimately becomes a Portal for your customers to the WWW.
Enhances team values	• Educate departments with courseware on-line, so saving off-site training costs.
Allows you to get 'closer' to what staff really think	• Set up regular on-line staff and supplier 'suggestion' discussions
Supports your recruitment drive	• Advertise job vacancies on the Web or integrate web advertising with paper-based campaigns • Contract specialist web employment agencies.

WEB FACTS

THE TYPICAL BRITISH FAMILY IS MORE LIKELY TO OWN A
COMPUTER THAN A DOG.

Reach higher

There are five steps towards securing a successful 'web
buyer' relationship.

1 dotcom suspect
In theory, just about anyone – unless too old or young –
could be in the market for your products or services. But
who?

2 dotcom prospect
The most lucrative way to identify good prospects, is
probably already on your desk. Perhaps you have boxes of
completed customer enquiry coupons gathering dust. Email
those prospects. If you haven't got an email address, try a
fax or telephone number. Reward prospects for providing
details and regularly check that your customer data is
'clean'; in other words, *up to date*. You can buy email listings
from specialist brokers. To draw in prospects, use a
combination of traditional advertising and Web marketing
such as the use of strategically placed banner ads.

3 dotcom customer

Your imaginative advertising and promotions secure a customer sale. Each time a surfer requests information about your organisation, in effect they are giving you the green light to conduct business with them. So why only use its basic features? Encourage ongoing relationships with your organisation. Perhaps, once they have made an initial purchase, you could offer a second product or service from your portfolio at a reduced price. Invite customers to visit your 'sister' brand sites: *secure that second sale*.

4 dotcom client

Now you're really into webmarketing. Efforts are beginning to pay off. Yet even securing a dotcom client status is not enough to complete the dotcom customer value cycle.

5 dotcom patron

If you reach this stage, your dotcom customer strategy is a total success. A patron will recommend your outstanding service to others. As these new prospects actively seek you rather than vice versa, you automatically skip the first 'suspect' stepping stone. In fact, if the patron is so enthusiastic about your service, the newly recruited prospect may start his or her relationship with your organisation as a dotcom customer.

Reward patrons who spread the word on your behalf. The more people whom they can recommend the greater the mutual benefits. To ensure fair play, all the patron has to do is provide an email contact for the new business prospect. Once the prospect becomes a customer, the patron is rewarded.

From brochureware to customer awareness

In Monday's section, we saw that many e-commerce businesses initially used the Web for brochureware. This step is aimed at those dotcom suspects we've just looked at. Getting people to browse through brochureware can be encouraged through traditional advertising, search engine marketing or good old fashion word-of-mouth. Once they've seen your brochureware, your audience will invariably demand more substance from your site.

The second stage is the information 'push' channel. Push technology can be likened to the dating game. You could either wait all night to make a move on your intended date or take the initiative through starting a conversation. If your opening gambit isn't sufficiently planned and styled you could end up dateless, spending the rest of the evening chewing on cheese puffs in the kitchen. Through empowering the person you want to 'chat-up', push technology puts you in control. He or she calls the shots for information, rather than you being forced into making an unsolicited approach.

This is great for customer support issues. Take the example of phone helplines. You can manage your customer support traffic by logging which enquiries attract the most 'hits'. Alternatively, you can feature a Web-customer support site in conjunction with a traditional phone-support site, thereby offering greater choice and further promoting a personalised service.

Finally, you can use 'kiosk-enabled' technology. This is embraced by organisations like local authorities who want to reach the community at the touch of a button: from offering on-line payment of community tax, to delivering the latest jobs from a strategically placed kiosk at either a town centre or bus shelter, for example. Such advances provide a novel advertising medium for webmarketers.

A safer sale

People increasingly 'click and buy'. It saves time and hassle. However, the more clicks you request, the more reasons for surfers to 'click out' and move onto a less tedious site. So sell from the first click.

Web technology can go a long way to guaranteeing a no-fuss sale. In the past, to close a sale most companies offered a telephone number or a fax service. As any salesperson can tell you, once customers leave the premises, you have an uphill struggle to get them back. Today most companies offer secure on-line credit card payment services. This is made safe through technology called Secure Socket Layer Protocols which scrambles information to and from a computer over the open Internet.

Internet security concerns often centre on the confidentiality and integrity of data whilst in transit over the network. As the volume of Internet commerce rises, so the need has grown for virtual equivalents of real world commercial validity protection such as signatures, contracts, authorisation, liability, and dispute resolution. Digital signatures use security technology to provide certification and to offer a guarantee that the surfer is whom he or she claims to be.

Some webmarketers offer on-line research for a limited time trial. This is fine, but credit card details are usually requested up front before any research can be conducted. The idea is that charges are debited only if and once the surfer decides to purchase the full service. More often than not this technique puts off more people than it attracts.

Web tip
Always feature your regular postal address on the site. Also, without consistent marketing no one will know that you're Web-active.

Hold your customers' hands
Having secured your e-customers, ask what they feel about your site. In so doing, you can build and segment specific customer profiles. Each group's comments contribute

PRACTICE SAFE SALES

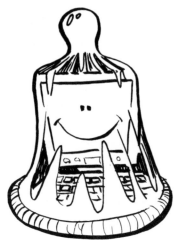

towards developing your Web presence by clarifying and enlightening your own ideas on ways and means to tailor your service.

The dotcom community

Call it the global or web village – both suggest a sense of community. Successful communities live and work in partnership. Your 'customer facing' site is a micro community of customers and suppliers. Help customers help each other via chat rooms and bulletin boards. Let them share a communal rapport with other communities. This could include offering freebies like T-shirts featuring your site, mouse mats – anything that helps spread not just the news that you are on-line but the feeling of good will. And remember, when a dotcom Patron gets in touch you should reply, not simply out of courtesy but with the aim to

show that you are listening, reacting and collaborating to
ensure a sustainable value-added web relationship.

wEB FACTs

WHEN EMAILED BY POTENTIAL CUSTOMERS, 50% OF UK
COMPANIES DID NOT RESPOND TO A REQUEST FOR INFORMATION.
OF THOSE THAT DID, AROUND ONE THIRD DID NOT PERSONALISE
RESPONSES. (SOURCE: UNIVERSITY OF WEST OF ENGLAND)

Putting it briefly

What are your dotcom marketing objectives? For example,
informing customers about your new e-service, preparing
and adapting your marketing collateral, updating your
customer support systems and so on. Put all these
requirements – and more – onto paper.

Your webmarketing position
Your site reflects your organisation's personality. Like all
personalities, it is multi-faceted, offering different qualities
of service to different types of customers. Over time, these
qualities mature. As a regular marketer, you ensure that
your traditional advertising consistently reflects your
personality. So the first impressions you make with
customers mirror your organisation's inner strengths. This
logic must be carried throughout your webmarketing-
positioning plan. Through distinguishing your dotcom
goals you can look at: Web business objectives, Web market
objectives, Web competitive strategy.

Web business planning brief

Your dotcom business objectives

1. Why do you want to go on the Web?

2. Are your competitors on the Web?

3. Rate out of three, the applications used by your competitors, e.g. brochureware.

4. What business aspect do you want the Web to address?

   For example:
   - Lead generation
   - Departmental integration
   - Stock control
   - Product distribution

   For each of these aspects, what results do you anticipate in the:

   i) short term?   ii) mid term?   iii) longer term?

Your enterprise-wide web objectives

5. Who, at which stage and at what level of involvement, from planning to implementation and finally support, will need an input into your web plan? The following checklist will help to identify the relevant factors within your organisation.

Department	Planning (level: 1–4)	Implementation (level: 1–4)	Support (level: 1–4)	Who holds ultimate department responsibility?
Recruitment				
Finance				
Sales				
Distribution				
Brand marketing				
Product marketing				
Customer care				
Purchasing				
Corporate management				
Administration				
Research and development				
Training				

It is essential that you have the appropriate business financial systems to successfully manage your site. Seek advice from an e-commerce accountancy specialist who can explain the implications of local country tax and financial planning issues.

The fuller webmarketing brief

This self-contained brief covers every key question for developing a creative webmarketing solution.

1. Who's going Web-wide?
Company name only. Other facts should be confined to a section called 'Background'.

2. Describe what you do
Telecoms, Financial, Manufacturing etc.

3. What should your budget cover?

- Site design
- Technical support
- Web-marketing
- Site copy
- Traditional support marketing

Remember: part of your budget should be set aside for unforeseen items.

4. In terms of site style, do you need:

- a new information site?
- an interactive site?
- a customer facing site?
- an internal market site?
- a business-to-business site?
- a combination of some or all of the above?

Would you consider:

- Incentiveware, e.g. free shareware (payment free software)?

- Screensavers, chat rooms?
- Databases of previously published e-zines, newsletters or data sheets?

5. Who will administer the site?
Do you need a specialised Web Master, i.e. a person who oversees the site?

6. Who will host the site?
See the section in Wednesday's chapter on ISPs and IHPs

7. Will you need multi-media CD ROM/DVD?

- With interactive access to the Web
- Stand alone

8. Web banner ads

- Why advertise?
- Should it be Web-marketed to other sites?
- Would you consider swapping banner ads with other related companies?
- Where should a banner ad lead, i.e. who hosts the end site?
- Should the Web banner be animated? If so by means of which language?
  (Bear in mind platform interoperability issues)
- How much do you want to spend on your banner ad?
- How will you measure the response to a banner add? For example number of impressions (times it appears over a fixed period) or actual clicks.

9. Media/PR access link

- How often will news be updated?

- Do you need a journalist 'hot-link' email button?
- Will you offer a repository of press-releases and/or sound or video clips?

10. What do you specifically expect your site to achieve? By which of the following will you measure success?

- Return visits to the site
- Sales
- Postal savings
- Depth of knowledge discovered via e-forms
- Brand awareness
- Savings on existing commercial infrastructure
- Customer referrals/ leads
- Savings in paper-work
- Redirected enquiries via hypertext links and referrals
- Captured email details
- Savings in human resources
- PR
- Awards for your site
- Distribution/asset management cost savings, eg via on-line auctions

In relation to your existing marketing plan what are your:

1   Webmarketing tactical objectives?
2   Corporate strategic objectives?

11. About your Web community

- How Internet aware is your community?
- How often do they connect?
- Demographics
- Reasons for connecting?

Typical surfers connecting to your dotcom business:

- Staff
- Salespeople
- Distribution channel
- Retailers
- Journalists
- Suppliers
- Potential employees
- Shareholders
- Lobbyists
- Schools
- Students
- Partners

Name two requirements of each group.

12. How do you see yourself?
What style should the look and copy for your site adopt eg serious, casual?

13. What supporting media will you use to promote your site?
For example, national newspapers, PR trade press. In all cases, try and include a sample.

13a. Why did you opt for this media?

14. What Web marketing methods will you consider?

- *Meta-tags*: HTML – Hyper Text Transfer Protocol description labels which are 'read' by search engines
- *WWW advertising*: including banner advertising – small display ads on a site which, when 'clicked', link to your site
- Search engine marketing
- Links to other sites: via hypertext links which, when 'clicked', jump from the original page to another site or page
- Newsgroups: a public forum or discussion area on the Web
- Recipient approved email
- On-line journalists

- Internal training
- Web rings: similar to Newsgroups, a band of home pages, with the same subject, grouped together by an organisation
- Mini sites modified in content according to target groups. These sites appear on appropriate complementary partner sites.

15. When do you expect to see:

- A draft?
- A published site?
- The support marketing campaign?
- The technical infrastructure?

Finally, sign off the brief. This binds you and your supplier to getting the project done as agreed and to a deadline.

Sites tend to grow in content according to the amount of time you spend building them. Time, especially when dealing with Web designers, is money. So agree everything on paper before committing to a Web publishing stage.

Never be tempted to squeeze additional last minute material into your site, especially after the initial contents have been agreed. You will exceed your budget and may compromise the integrity of your site's design.

Web tip

What are competitive sites offering? What is easy to download? Could you combine features from separate sites? How would you improve a feature? What would you design into your site that your competitors haven't?

Armed with this information, get yourself a roll of cheap plain wallpaper and flow-chart your site. Start with the first page.

- Indicate the number of featured pages, varying text throughout the site.
- Show links to other sites, i.e. hypertext links.
- Never offer too many links per page.
- Consider a permanent site flow chart on each page.

Back to the drawing board. Draw up a rough layout of each page, or an electronic draft version.

Samples of website layouts

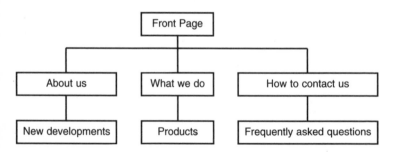

Basic website structure

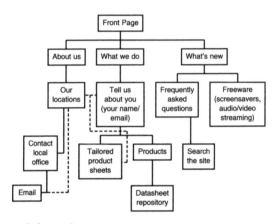

Basic customer dialogue site

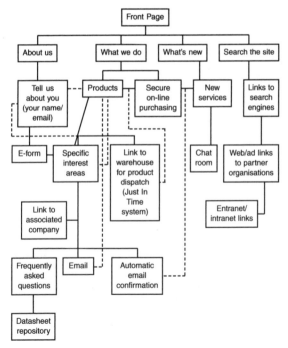

Basic sales website

Establishing a site: some golden rules

- Ask someone not associated with your company for views on what makes a good site
- Establish what your site should accomplish before you start
- Make sure your site is relevant to your business
- Make sure your site features useful information
- Keep your site up-to date and spellchecked
- If possible make your site interactive
- Consider including a leisure aspect to your site
- Don't make your site too complicated to navigate
- Leave some budget for unforeseen changes
- Anticipate changes to your site format
- Develop your changes according to site performance
- Promote, promote, promote using traditional advertising and marketing techniques.

Establishing your position

Many organisations get their Web mission confused with their Web positioning. A mission is your vision of the future:

Within two years, we intend to switch our retail operation from traditional high street trading to 24–7 e-commerce.

Web goals adapt to changing long term circumstances. Once you have achieved your goals consider new missions and objectives.

Your positioning mirrors how your current dotcom service embraces targeted market needs, typically:

- What your site offers?
- How your Intranet/Extranet supports that offer?
- Why the offer is so special?
- How else you'll deliver a complete dotcom solution?

From position to mission

Position	Position	Mission	Mission
What you do	What you deliver	Where you want to be	Your perfect scenario, ideal position, ultimate achievement
Why you do it	How you deliver	How you intend to get there	

Solid ⟶ fluid

Questions to consider in your web positioning plan

1 **Why are you going on-line?** To reach a wider audience – to improve distribution cycles, to extend your connected enterprise to suppliers and partners and to gain greater control of your internal processes.

2 **How does Web-enabled technology enhance your business?** Your site delivers an easy way to order catering equipment, for example, or your Intranet offers greater management control.

3 **What makes your Web strategy a WOW! tactic?** Your WEBA: **W**eb, **E**nabled, **B**usiness, **A**dvantage.

For example, are you more Web savvy than your competitors? (WEBAs replace traditional Unique Selling Points)

Above all, for whom is your web business intended?

What specifically does this audience want?

Why should yours be the only Web business of choice?

What arguments can you add to substantiate your position?

Summary

- Establish a relationship with e-customers – make your site more valuable than 'brochureware'
- Explore ways to assure security for surfers – especially if you are going to sell on the Web
- Prepare a web brief for outside creative suppliers
- Delegate to key personnel specific responsibility for your web plan
- Turn the average site into a WOW! site through following the golden rules and WEBA.

Your web home
Internet hosting providers

In the short term, getting the right hardware and software for your dotcom business may seem costly. However, in terms of longer-term savings covering every aspect from infrastructure to paperwork, the scenario may look a lot more encouraging. Plus, you have to consider the costs of your business being off-line if things are not sufficiently pre-planned.

HOME SWEET WWW

Server solutions need to scale according to your business needs. Beacon Group in Australia and Japan leads the world in Web-enabled temporal database management software such as Timecube which pin-points and tracks the historical performance of individual items in your database.

Others offer relational databases, tools and application products, all vital for your web business plans.

In the right hands and with the right support, you can expand your e-commerce and open computing tactics from being a cost centre platform to a profit base, embracing selling, taking secure payments, encouraging customer/supplier relationships and reducing the buying cycle.

Web tip

If your customers prefer the option of secure Web payments, set up a special secure server and payment software program. At the very least, offer surfers the chance to print out a completed order form and fax or post it back. (A word of caution – don't copy the design of your non-web order form to the Web. You would be amazed at how many Web order forms feature the instructions, 'Please tear here'!)

Managing your network

Diffusing your web business access amongst a network of several servers is called 'server farming'.

Apart from the expense of hardware and software, there is the cost of employing someone to manage your network. Depending on the size of your operation and the depth of your pockets, you can either pay for an on-site engineer or let an external host cover costs. Having your server and engineer on-site means you literally see everything as it happens. Providing of course that someone is there when 'it' does.

For example, if it's 3 am on a public holiday and your server goes down, it may still take hours to get into the office, assess the damage and then resolve the problem. On the other hand, if your site was hosted externally with a big Internet Service Provider you could spread the cost of hiring and action would be taken quickly.

Also keep in mind the outlay of installing and maintaining a host's main data cable into your premises. Many believe that the cost is justifiable as it speeds up network access times for employees. In theory, the bigger the bandwidth, the greater the amount of data. In practice it's how you manipulate the bandwidth.

To ensure your site remains efficient and reactive, instal a separate cable for secure, swift staff email surfing, leaving all the bandwidth on your other line for your main site.

Internet Hosting Providers (IHPs)

Internet Hosting Providers (IHPs) feature Virtual Web Servers. These computers offer access to several dedicated sites on one server. As there are only a restricted number of sites per server, you gain from an *a la carte* hosting service. You can load software remotely, as well as allow a host server to run programs on your behalf as an integral element of your Web connection on any kind of operating system. Arguably, with this option, only limitations are the amount of space allocated on a host server and on your disc drive.

One step beyond

If you prefer not to share server space with other organisations but equally you don't want to take up valuable office space with your own servers, consider co-hosting with an IHP. Your site will be located and monitored at your host's main Internet access building. You can gain secure access to the server and negotiate to pay by the number of hits (volume of customer interest) you receive, or a flat fee that allows for unlimited traffic. This is one step below actually becoming your own ISP. Today, the option of being your own ISP isn't as expensive as you may believe. You can negotiate to market your own ISP name as a joint venture with an existing IHP or telecoms provider. This means that you can send out your own branded internet connection software which offers free Web access. Once the IHP or telecom company has made an agreed commission from the initial telephone calls to your service, you too can take a percentage share in future dial-up access telephone fees.

Final check list

Before taking the final plunge with any IHP, draw up a checklist:

- Traffic: Is there a restriction to the number of hits you can have? If so what are the extra costs?
- How much disk space can you have? For a powerful site look for anything from 50 Mb upwards.
- Can you have your own domain name?
- What if you want to move your site – are there any penalties?
- What kind of host service commitment can you anticipate?
- Can you speak to other customers?
- Can your host deal with all operating systems, including Mac, UNIX, Windows and NT?
- Can you personalise software for benefits like processing order forms (Common Gateway Interface

scripts which let you interface programs on your PC with servers, so you can add site information as you please)?

• Can you upload designs/new data to the site?
• Do you have to pay separately for email?
• If you are dealing with an overseas country, does the host offer tailored local connections?
• Can the provider cope with geographic time differences and local peak demands?
• Is the provider in for the long term or quick profit (this will affect service contracts)?
• Can the provider support developments like Web TV?
• Does your host offer 'multihoming', i.e. more than one main link to the Web? This is essential: if one link fails other resources keep your site on-line.
• Can you get regular site visit reports?

Internet Service Providers (ISPs)

Also known as Internet Access Providers, these offer dial-up services connecting your organisation to the World Wide Web. Many also offer a hosting service, but this is not their main source of revenue. Providers managing infrastructure and bandwidth are called Internet Platform Providers.

Types of dial up service
If your company needs to connect no more than five PCs to the Web (mainly for email, for instance), consider a standard 56 Kb modem connection per PC, over a standard phone line. Or for faster traffic or to use the phone and email on the same line, perhaps a 128Kb connection; split by 64 Kb and 64 Kb. Either way, you pay a monthly subscription that covers unlimited Internet access. Broad

band access is becoming, in the UK, more readily available and is set to become the standard.

In its favour, a regular monthly subscription is a cost-effective way to get connected. Apart from a phone point and modem there is no other hardware commitment. On the downside, though:

- it can be difficult to track site visitors
- phone bills can swell, especially with lots of accounts
- support can be sketchy
- unless you have a friendly ISP, updating your site contents can be difficult at best or impossible at worst.

Go with the flow

Once you connect over five computers, seriously consider investing in an Integrated Subscribers Digital Network (ISDN) supported by a router. If you want to send large graphic files to designers or printers, you really cannot do without an ISDN. Other benefits include:

- instant connections and disconnections, saving cost and time.
- a network of up to forty PCs can be connected to one ISDN line and still operate unremittingly
- you can allocate individual PC web addresses, perfect for guiding traffic as well as internal email systems.

You could consider installing a dedicated high speed leased line. You pay for the line, not the charges, which guarantees a steady connection. Owning the line means you can dispense with an ISP. On the downside, weigh the costs (which are high) against your Web usage. Firewalls (security software) will have to be incorporated as your company is directly linked to the World Wide Web. You'll also need either to employ or have access to someone who can maintain your line 24–7.

The bigger your bandwidth the broader your marketing potential Webbrand leaders offer the biggest bandwidth – and thus the greatest Web service.

Something for nothing?

An ISP often provides free Web space along with free email addresses and other goodies such as website statistics, tailored Portals (see section on Portals), community chat-rooms and on-line help.

However, you don't own a clearly personal Web address. Instead your address becomes part of the ISP's Web address such as **theworks@freespace.net** (these sites are called 'sub domains' or 'non virtual' accounts). Should you decide to move onto another service provider, you'll have to re-register your site: a nuisance when having to inform all of your customers about the new address.

Demand more from your Internet Service Provider
You are spoilt for ISP choice. Don't automatically opt for the biggest or most expensive ISP. The more people connected to an ISP the greater the potential for Web congestion. On the other hand, the more people connected to an ISP, the greater the chance that customers are happy with the service. Take your choice!

In addition to the standard ISP services, your provider may offer one or more of the following:

- Website development and training
- E-commerce such as electronic storefronts and on-line information services
- Intranet/Extranet hosting
- On-line marketing support
- Database hosting
- Premium network services; including Virtual Private Networks (VPNs)
- Reselling of hardware and software to corporate clients
- Voice over IP (the digital low cost, Web-enabled alternative to traditional telephone services).

When you've got to go

Service and disk space are the main reasons why people move sites from ISPs and IHPs. If and when you decide to move the transition should be made easier by taking the following measures:

First, obtain a written agreement that permits release from the ISP's service within a timeframe convenient to your business.

Secondly, make sure you check and complete all relevant paperwork regarding the responsibility for the technical, administrative and financial aspects of your domain. If your domain name ends with .co.uk, .ltd or .plc, register details with an organisation called Nominet (*www.nominet.org.uk*). Come what may, you'll officially own the domain. And as with most other legal aspects of this ilk, ownership is nine tenths of the law. If you wish to register a dotcom address, amongst the places to try is *www.com-domains.com/*

Thirdly, always keep a back-up copy of your site on disc.

When it comes to moving the domain, simply inform the incumbent provider and successor, co-ordinate a day and time for the move, making sure your address provider is given sufficient notice – and then move.

Domain name 'landgrab'

Eventually, the Web will have to replace domain names with domain numbers. If not, the names will just get longer and longer. Today, www.sex.com is so profitable (with over nine million registered members) that it allegedly charges webmarketers $1 million to place a monthly banner ad on the site. www.drugs.com cost its owners $200,000 to buy. www.wallstreet.com sold for $1.03 million. However, numerous new suffixes are now available which could free up web name space. For example .biz and .net.

Summary

Today you learned to choose the appropriate means to connect to the Web for your business. Remember – consider the volume of anticipated Web traffic. Do you need to guarantee Web connect 24–7? Do you need to send documents more substantial than word processed email – if so you'll need ISDN or consider ADSL or even 3G technology – and can you afford to host a server on site?

Web research

For an effective webmarketing plan, you need to understand:

- Who wants your product or service?
- Why would they venture into webspace to find it?
- How can you prevent them from 'clicking' with your competitors?

The more you ask, the more you'll need to ask. Such as, what is the potential value of your web market? If you aim to sell, which of your products already performs well in a direct marketing context? All these affect your web marketplace. What about your web strategy?

- How will webmarketing affect the end cost to the consumer?
- What are the best ways to control distribution?
- How do you exploit local issues globally?
- How will you manage customer support programmes?
- Can you provide an effective dotcom service?
- How do your competitors fair in all of this?

Published web research

Various firms produce web reports covering everything from who's on-line, to why they use the Internet. Report prices vary depending on their accuracy. There are also some on-line companies who are happy to offer basic reports free of charge. They do this as part of their own webmarketing strategy. The

free reports or newsletters encourage visits to the report writers' main site or to the sites of interest covered in the newsletter. Some enterprising webmarketers charge the featured sites for the privilege to be included in the distributed email reports.

Search engine research

The most common method of research is via search engines. There are thousands of such engines on the Web, yet only a few are used extensively.

Turbo charged research

The basic way to find a subject is to enter your keywords (in lower case format) in the 'SEARCH FOR' box, click the search icon and wait for the results. Then click on the link provided (underlined and in colour) which takes you to the site. Note that inputing in lower case finds both the lower and upper case versions of your desired subject.

If you want a specific word included in your search, put a plus (+) sign in front of the keyword in the search box:

creativity + works

To exclude a word and hence refine your search, place a minus (−) sign before the unnecessary word in the search box:

creativity + works − art

To enhance your search with different endings, type an asterix (*) at the end of the keyword:

Wish* − also finds wishes, wishful, wishbone, wishy-washy

Many search engines feature multiple choice, 'tick box' driven searches. However, some like AltaVista offer deeper searching abilities.

You type . . .

domain:domainname	Finds pages with a specific domain
domain:org	Finds organisation pages
host:name	Finds pages on a specific computer
host:jonathan.theworks.co.uk	
	Finds pages on an individual PC called Jonathan at the works.co.uk
image:filename	Finds pages with images with a specific file name, eg image: menorah – finds all pictures of menorahs
link:URLtext	Finds pages containing the specified text in any part of the page other than an image, link or URL

title:text	Finds pages containing specific words or a phrase in the page title
URL:text	Finds pages with a specific word or phrase in the title
applet:calculator	Finds pages using applets (a free application program that performs a simple task) called calculator

Lap top research

The best source of on-line research is to ask for views from your existing circle of customers and associates as well as employees and suppliers. Surfers hate to waste time completing forms, so design a questionnaire which ensures uncompleted questions don't hold up form processing through re-posting, ie asking again for the form to be completed because of lack of information.

Next, think about why you are asking surfers to complete a questionnaire. What will they and you gain? Reassure surfers that answers are confidential, including a confidentiality clause before and after your questions. If you intend to use the answers for other divisions within your company, offer your respondents the option of declining to share their data with other related services (if any division is a separate company, normally, under the Data Protection Act, you are prohibited in the UK from sharing data without the correspondent's permission). For example: **This Net survey is anonymous. Answers are never written to disk. Plus of course we have no idea of your real identity. So please answer honestly.**

If specifically cited at the end of the research session, you may offer respondents a sales brochure on behalf of the company commissioning the research. But beware: covert, 'pushy' selling via Web research isn't just illegal but, from a marketing point of view, stupid. You'll probably alienate more potential customers instead of recruiting them.

Planning your questions
Make your first question easy, completing a sample question to show how to answer the rest of the questionnaire.

Ask one question at a time, eg NOT **Do you have a PC and MAC?**

Try whenever possible, to avoid open-ended questions, eg **Will the Internet become more important to business than retail space?**

Opt for simple words rather than convoluted ones. eg NOT **expostulate** – instead **argue**.

Whenever possible avoid leading questions, eg **Do you surf at work because it is cheaper than surfing at home?**

Don't intimidate surfers, eg **Do your work mates think you're cool?**

WEB FACTS

BRMB INTERNATIONAL RESEARCH REVEALS THAT OF THOSE WHO ARE ON-LINE, 42% OF PEOPLE IN THE UK ACCESS THE WEB FROM HOME, WHILE 38% GO ON-LINE FROM THE WORKPLACE

Always offer a choice of answers to specific questions, including a NOT APPLICABLE option, eg **Do you have a Single PC [] More than one PC [] Are part of a network [] None of the above []**

Be wary of semantics. Don't use language which reflects your personal views, eg neither **Geek** nor **WebHead**. Rather **Web technologist**

Include a '**Don't know**' option where applicable. If the surfer doesn't have an opinion he or she may give up on your entire questionnaire. There are no 'right' answers. Assure your respondent you are assessing your product or service – not the surfer.

Limit the range of your questions. Rather than: **How many e-zines do you subscribe to?** ask about each of the e-zine categories by sector, one at a time and then: **In a month** do you get email from **one [ ] two [ ] three [ ] e-zines?**

You can be guided further on how to ask a general research question by studying Teach Yourself Imaginative Marketing (Hodder & Stoughton Educational).

wEB FACTs

ACCORDING TO FORRESTER RESEARCH, 60% OF THOSE WEB VISITORS WHO START AN ORDER FORM NEVER COMPLETE IT. A GROWING TREND TO COMBAT THIS LETHARGY IS TO OFFER SURFERS A 'PHONE ME' BUTTON. THE WEBMARKETER RECEIVES THE SURFER'S DETAILS, THEN CALLS BACK VIA A REGULAR TELEPHONE LINE.

Virtual Brainstorming™

One type of Web research is called Virtual Brainstorming™
(VB). Devised by *gabaynet*, it uses the Web as well as other
media to generate an appropriate physical and
psychological environment for solving problems. For
example, rather than surfers just completing a
questionnaire, they can explore a specially designed
research site, 'click' on items of interest, answer a few
questions – and control the research. All of this is supported
by focus groups using creative problem solving
methodologies.

VB media range from global conference-type links between
participants, to the utilisation of Virtual Reality Modelling
Languages, including Java and related 'Write Once – Use
Anywhere' software. VB sessions may feature the physical
simulation of either the specific problem to be brainstormed
or areas relating to the problem. Typically, this would
include the orchestration of sight, taste or touch. In all
instances, VB features the talents of a trained facilitator,
project co-originator and designer.

Web consumer targeting

Despite many dotcoms turning into notcoms, today, in the
UK alone, over ten million consumers have direct access to
the Internet.

The stereotypical surfer is male, 35 years old, financially
secure and living in a house without children. Male ABC1s
UK Internet penetration is approaching 50%. This is
obviously an extremely sizeable and key potential market,

but with so many people converging onto the Web generally, you need to rationalise how you segment a target audience.

How many on-line?

Based on published surveys, an 'educated guess' as to how many are on-line worldwide by mid 2003 is 200 million. These figures take into account that only 15% of the world's population contain 88% of all the Internet users whilst 80% of the world's population hasn't even used a telephone.

Sex

The broadest way to segment a Web audience is by sex. In the early 2000's, male surfers outnumbered female surfers by four to one – now the numbers are close to being level, with women accounting for around 43% of the UK market (Source: MORI). According to NetSmart, 88% of US women said the Web simplifies their lives. 83% said it saves time.

55% go on-line because it saves money. 81% of women said they don't know how they survived without the Internet.

In the UK, the growth of the Web has impacted on traditional segmentation methods to such an extent that the government has suggested dividing socio-economic groups into a hierarchy of job categories.

Web tip
Email can double as an advertisement. Simply add a 'signature' file message (found under the preferences section of your email program). Type any message you wish. Each time you send an email the 'advertisement' follows. This is especially effective when participating in newsgroup discussions.

Newsgroups
To get closer to your web audience visit a newsgroup. There are thousands on-line. Each forum of surfers has specialised interests including your organisation's field. Through earning respect by targeted newsgroups – no more than eight really good ones – you can understand your market's character and with permission from the newsgroup controller, conduct informal research.

Web rings

Your site probably offers similar products and services to many others. Rather than fight the competition, why not join a Web ring? This is a collection of links with a common theme or interest which is actively sought by would-be customers via search engines. To find one that's suitable for you go to www.webring.org. Alternatively, start up your own, profiting from inviting other sites to link to your site.

WEB FACTS

RESEARCH ESTIMATES THAT BY 2004 TEENAGERS WILL GENERATE $2 BN IN ON-LINE PURCHASES. CHILDREN AGED 5 TO 12 WILL SPEND $100M. BY 2005 THERE WILL BE AROUND 77 MILLION UNDER 18'S ON-LINE GLOBALLY. IN BRITAIN, A STUDY BY NOP RESEARCH FOUND THAT, SOCIALLY, SURFERS ARE DESCRIBED BY TEENAGERS AND CHILDREN (WITH AND WITHOUT INTERNET ACCESS), AS 'CLEVER', 'FRIENDLY', 'COOL', 'TRENDY' AND 'RICH'.

Summary

- Target your research
- Construct your on-line questionnaire with care
- Market to newsgroups and Web rings
- Check out Web-published material through search engines
- Consider the virtues of Virtual Brainstorming
- Pinpoint the characteristics of your surfers and serve them appropriately.

Web copy

Your surfers simply don't have the time to trawl through a densely worded website or email for valuable marketing propositions. Once people have logged onto your site your words need to keep them hooked. Vary the shape of the words on the screen. If a screen looks like a congested car park, you'll lose surfer traffic. Give words the space to breathe.

A common webcopy mistake is to incorporate hypertext links into the middle of a sentence. Through clicking on the link, your reader never completes your sentence. You quite literally waste your words. Moreover, as in all forms of writing, people naturally read the beginning of your web copy, then lose interest, only to regain interest towards the end. There is a simple way to keep your audience alert, and the clue is in your hands. This book is divided into seven days. That means seven separate triggers of interest. The more you can subdivide your message into readable chunks, the greater the chance of retaining a hold on your potential customers' minds.

Open minds – open opportunities

Whenever writing a business letter, you should try to keep your reader's thoughts open. The same applies to web copy. The end of a paragraph signifies the end of a specific thought. That could be misinterpreted as the end of a message. The trick is to link each thought so that together they become a train of ideas.

'Open reading' is particularly challenging on the Web. When your surfer watches a screen (which they read from the

centre outwards), there's nothing to fold up (like a piece of paper). Once the surfer gets distracted or tired, he or she is likely either to click out of your page or literally switch off. One way to avoid 'closed reading' is to feature link phrases that encourage the surfer to read further and longer:

'But ...'	'What's more ...'
'However ...'	'In addition ...'

You can also use Web technology such as animated GIFS (pictures) to lead the surfer through your site. Unlike any other form of advertising, webmarketing technology delegates final control of content to your audience, so it's not enough to invest in mass 'wall-papered' awareness of your message/brand. Instead, consider why a surfer would choose to read or access that message in the first place.

'Gluey bits' is a webmarketing expression relating to features and benefits that keep surfers 'stuck' to your site. Crucially, these will ensure that your site contents are current and appealing. Further suggestions include:

1 Feature a news section or updated database of useful facts.
2 Offer something a surfer can't get elsewhere – such as a special deal section.
3 Link to a site offering ready-made 'gluey bits' such as a financial newspaper's stock market page (speak to the paper for costs).
4 Offer rewards just for visiting your site (great to elicit email addresses).
5 Personalise page preferences.
6 Intrigue with an interactive game or competition.

Have you read this?

Daily you listen or see up to 200 orders: 'mind the gap', 'visit this site' and so on. Twenty per cent are forgotten. So avoid noise where a confluence of messages drowns out the thrust of your well-intentioned argument.

Another potential downside of snappy web copy is that we are becoming a nation of e-literates, uncaring for

Web tip
Competition rules vary depending on your server's location. If it is in the UK you may have to consider restricting entrants to UK citizens. EU regulations apply if you want to make your competition Euro-wide. You can learn more about competition and prize draw rules by studying Teach Yourself Creative Advertising and Copywriting, published by Hodder & Stoughton Educational.

grammatical style. So revert to the craft of getting your message intelligently read. Rely on fundamental truths as practised in traditional direct mail copy:

Attention leads to Interest, Interest leads to Desire, Desire leads to the need for Conviction, and Conviction leads to Action. (**AIDCA**). Paramount in this equation is Conviction. Unless you can *convince* your web audience of your proposition's value, webcopy is just marketing 'garnish'. Today's audience can see beyond the pomp: they want attainable benefits.

Web tip
Follow up an email or completed e-form within 24 hours. Any longer and you widen the gap towards securing a websale.

Web-grabbing words and phrases
Assess the following sentences:

A) Activate words and sentences – seize your surfers' attention.

B) The more active your words and sentences, the higher the probability of retaining your surfers' attention throughout.

Which sentence did you prefer?

Webmarketing email 'grab' phrases like 'read this before your next coffee break' are often a good bet. But use them liberally to complement rather than replace a solid benefit-led proposition.

- Are you ready for this?
- Hate work?
- Want to meet your match?
- Do you really need to read this?
- Here's what you've been waiting for
- Save direct
- Haven't we met?
- Your competitor wants this kept secret
- I wish someone had told me ...
- Don't you just hate email?

Avoid innuendo in email headings. For example:

To: (name of recipient)
RE: Suck my pen ...

The surfer opens the message which reveals:

Sometimes, work gets me so frustrated that when I suck my office pen, I swallow the ink! If you have days like these, you'll be interested to learn about our brand new ...

Also, avoid overt capitalisation in emails: OVER EMPHASIS LOSES IMPACT and upper case is equivalent to shouting, whilst *Italics* or **bold** is likely to lose format on the surfer's browser.

Beware vapourware
Vapourware is a type of software or website that promises much but delivers very little. Instead aim for substance in your copy. Simply explain your product or service benefits: When can you deliver ... Can you offer a guarantee? ... Demonstrate a product's features and benefits through

words and in graphics if appropriate, including using animated technologies like Flash and Java. As with all forms of direct marketing, wherever possible use testimonials from satisfied customers: no other form of advertising does you greater credit than a personal recommendation.

Adding something new?
If you can't add anything new on the Web to your existing marketing material, endeavour to rewrite your brochure, as if it were a storyboard.

Instead of subheads, use Web-animated technology and graphics to introduce new text scenes. Treat each screen page as if it were the only one a surfer sees. In many cases your site will only be read superficially. That's why copy has to work hard. Even if you feature hypertext links, assume your surfers will never explore further. When and if they do, your efforts to maximise impact will be especially rewarding.

As with all story outlines, make sure that your site has a beginning (intro or overview), middle (content – with substance) and end (either directing surfers to a sales/enquiry e-form, or ensuring that you've covered everything they need to know). To ensure they reach a conclusion, don't be afraid to offer some kind of reward for their completed e-form. Also highlight urgency for their early response.

Finally, spellcheck your site. Better still, get others to spell-check it and never rely solely on a word-processing spellchecker program. You need to check sense as well as spelling!

Wave your banner

Apart from search engines and traditional marketing tools – including word of mouth – the most common Web advertising is the banner ad. Originally, these static oblongs featured a JPEG or PICT graphic of a company logo. When clicked, the banner linked to a webmarketer's site. Advertising revenues were, and still are, generated by the site hosting the banner. Nowadays, in addition to being animated through rich media content such as Java and Flash, banners are personalised. So, as well as being branding devices, they are also direct marketing tools.

Banner personalisation is achieved on two levels. First, via the environment where the banner appears. The more aligned the host site is to your market, the higher the chance of someone clicking the banner. Check that you can track your clicks either via a specialist Web agency or using software tracking systems.

Good places to feature banners include e-zine listings, newsletters and what I call hand in glove sites. These are webmarketers whose product or service complements yours. For example, an umbrella manufacturer and a weather forecaster. In either case, you feature a banner/personalised version of your site specific to surfers visiting the partner site.

You can also consider a part banner/part sponsorship of a site. For example, my own company, *gabaynet* (**www.theworks.co.uk**), was involved with a general Internet site for European soccer. The site was marketed as a sponsorship deal to webmarketers. The idea being that rather than webmarketers having to build their soccer site from scratch, one was ready-built. By advertising on it they gained from being associated with a popular sporting event and avoided paying costly sponsorship fees directly to the event's official organisers.

Secondly, consider banner personalisation – a banner ad featuring a personalised link of value. For example, some banners double up as 'phone me' buttons. The surfer completes basic email details, clicks the banner and receives a phone call from you.

You can join a free banner link network. Every time a surfer visits your site displaying a banner, you gain credits. After around two credits your banner is displayed on someone else's site.

Another technique is a free quotation based on some simple questions within the banner – for example, What's your name, age, are you a smoker? One click returns a basic life assurance quote. As you can imagine, the variations of this are endless. The only limits to banner flexibility – like most web creative issues – is bandwidth. The wider the bandwidth, the greater your creative possibilities.

One kind of banner ad that surfers either love or hate is the pop up box banner. This pops onto the screen whenever the surfer links to a specific site. It can either stay on the screen while the surfer continues browsing, 'flash' or stay a while and then fade. Pop up boxes – also known as Interstitial ads – are particularly effective as part of a search engine web marketing plan. The gateway appears before the engine sends a surfer to your site or a site related to the subject by keyword, dealt with by your organisation.

Superstitials, the next big thing in banner ads, feature Java-based rich media in any format: HTML, Director, Flash or

GIF. Unlike conventional banner ads, the superstitial does not load until the browser has loaded the entire page. Their cost to webmarketers can be up to four times the price of an ordinary banner, but they can yield up to twenty per cent better 'click through' rates.

Clicking for profit
The more popular the hosting site, and the more times your site appears, the bigger your banner budget (it's worth checking if your banner is going to be shown in rotation with other advertisers or 'fixed' to a specific page URL). Costs will modulate as more sites turn into portals. Another development, Web TV, with estimated audiences of 69 million in the US and Europe by 2005 (source: Datamonitor), may see the price of banner adds rocketing sky high or the price of traditional TV commercials falling. Even more so when, by 2015, TVs in homes may be 'hung' like wallpaper across entire walls, bringing a new dimension to the virtual world.

In the meantime, as an alternative to paying for a banner ad you could always host one – and still pick up valuable business.

An alternative to banner advertising is the Blipvert. Rather than sending a regular email, a 30-second audio clip of a sound track is attached. This idea is being adapted as part of 'signatures' at the bottom of emails. Often, Blipverts feature radio commercials or music excerpts.

Summary

Today we looked at the importance of grabbing phrases. You discovered why you shouldn't opt for the first banner ad offer someone tries to sell you. Finally, you've been encouraged to make your banner ad interactive.

Climbing higher

The discussion of how to improve your site search engine rankings has been left until last. Most people assume that the business of webmarketing is only about improving a site's visibility. As this book has shown, webmarketing touches *every* aspect of your organisation, not just the obvious. Here then are some tips to take your site to within the top 10 rankings and so further enhance its potential.

Most webmarketers have already had some Internet exposure and now want to make their sites work harder. Start by assessing what your peers think about your site. If they really like it, they'll link. Go to *www.yahoo.com* and type:

link: (your site address URL)

and you'll see just how many other sites link to yours. To tune up your site, from improving browser compatability to the overall design, go to www.websitegarage.com. This shows useful ways to tune up your site, from improving browser compatibility to the overall design. (When considering 'visibility', check how your site looks on different versions of browsers – some may not support your software, hinder printing or compromise graphics.)

Keywords open doors

Search engines rank sites using certain parameters. Some individual sites bid for keywords. Some engines rank according to a site's popularity and number of links. Most commonly, engines rank according to frequency and position of keywords. Every day engines catalogue billions of keywords using an algorithm. Ranking often depends on elements like domain name, document title, HTML page description, page position, frequency and pattern of words, sentence and paragraph structure and other HTML mark up considerations.

Choose your words, carefully repeat them often (especially in the first two paragraphs) but not excessively throughout the site. Wherever possible, turn keywords into plurals or nouns. These will throw up more findings. (*webmarketer* is better than *webmarketing*).

www.positionagent.com shows where your site actually lies in the hierarchy of search engine listings. This is assessed by either your URL or keywords related to your business.

Every Web page has its own coding. To see your HTML code whilst on the Web, go to 'File' and then view page source. This is full of meta-tags. Meta-tags are the backbone search support behind every site. Agree with your colleagues on suitably descriptive keywords, including associated words. Remember: if you are selling lots of models from a portfolio of goods, always involve the model number as many surfers will look for this first. Check that in the code line starting

```
<meta name = 'keywords' content =
```

you've added the appropriate words. Another tip is to try and feature a keyword within your domain name. This further improves your ranking. Engines take note of words with a major heading format. So use pre-set formats like

Heading 1, 2 and 3.

Although search engines reward extra ratings for nice graphics, without XML (see next page) their technology often cannot read pictures (that includes logos and features like animation). So, returning to your meta-tags, include an <u>alt tag</u> description wherever there's a picture. In this tag describe a benefit rather than simply writing – <u>graphic</u>. Bear in mind that the bigger your graphic file size, the longer the download. Try compressing your graphics, providing picture quality remains acceptable . If your site features an animated splashpage – featuring software such as Shockwave – surfers may not get to see it if they find your site via a search engine. As with the case of graphics, many search engine robots can't interpret frames or programs which surfers update when linking to the Internet (CGIs) – such as shopping carts. There are always new ways around this – consult your Web designer.

Engines can be pretty dumb, often providing inappropriate results, so label tags intelligently. If your order form features columns of information, make sure that each column has a meta-tag relating to its content as opposed to format.

Today, many web markets use XML (Extendible Mark-up Language). This tackles both Web content as well as categorising data according to agreed definitions. So 'Chips' would be signposted and made specific to either food or computers, 'The Times' would relate to a newspaper as opposed to clocks and so on. XML also helps PDAs and other Web connected devices decide whether to download or ignore a complex document.

Another overlooked part of a site – by people, not engines,

is the page title box. In this instance, in your meta-tags type:

<HTML> (head) (title) (words describing the page contents and, if you like, your company name)

and these will appear on the page title. Throughout your site, you can further improve rankings by adding a comment section in the meta tags.

< - - (Additional explanation of what you do) then close with -)

Get registered – but not too soon
Eighty five percent of surfers will find you via search engines like www.google.com. So search engine companies are busy. Keep them happy by only submitting your site once you are sure it's ready. Having said that, if you are going to break your site down by page, never send in too many pages from the same URL at once; instead spread it out. The engine personnel are busy, but sharp. So don't attempt sending in misleading meta-tag descriptions.

In addition to viewing your coding, search engines may rank according to:

- Loading speed – the faster the download, the higher the ranking
- Spelling – poor spelling may suggest poor service
- Colour of text – worth dabbling with but consistency tends to work best (some engines have been known to give credit for vivid colours)

- Number of good links in addition to links to other sites – which should be invited to link back to you. Always ensure that every sub-page within your site links back to your home page
- Relevance to subject – if your site is just a façade for something other than its category listing you will plummet down the rankings
- Value added features like chat rooms, e-zines and searchable databases.

Watching the competition

There are two sides to a chain's link. Here's the other half of the story. If your competitor is ranked higher than you, try the search engine 'link' technique on that site. Perhaps some of those links would like to couple up with you. If you want to find as many competitors as possible, apart from the ones you already know, go to your favourite engine and look for an option to 'find sites like this'.

Looking at your competitors' meta-tags, do they feature something that you don't? If everything is just about equal, you could find the problem is that you simply misspelt a few meta-tag keywords.

Well that's about it – for now. To share webmarketing tips with readers for future editions or catch up on the latest innovations, please visit www.gabaynet.com. You've learned a lot in just seven days – now take the next steps towards a successful webmarketing future for you and your organisation. Good luck!

Summary

1. Never forget: ultimately you are dealing with people, not computers.
2. People are social animals, so use the Web to unite communities throughout the global economy.
3. Build bridges between your organisation and all connecting to it using intra and extra networks.
4. News on the Web, good or bad, travels fast. Remain commercially aware and socially responsible.
5. No one will pay for anything on the Web until and unless you pay attention to them.
6. Web brands reflect what people need, not what you want – deliver and make their attainment rewarding.
7. It's no longer 'us and them', sales and marketing or IT and management: become a marketing communications *integrator*.
8. However far the Web reaches, land, sea or air, never lose sight that it's only as powerful as your original simple business objective.
9. Today's web technology is tomorrow's Morse code. If you can't enhance your webmarketing your strategy is misled and tactics out-dated.
10. Without consistent webmarketing, the average product life cycle of a website is just months.

email: jj@gabaynet.com

SUN
MON
TUE
WED
THU
FRI
SAT

For information

on other

IN A **WEEK** titles

go to

www.inaweek.co.uk